The Perfect Fundraiser

by Alison Reynolds

illustrated by Dylan Gibson

a Capstone company — publishers for children

Engage Literacy is published in the UK by Raintree.
Raintree is an imprint of Capstone Global Library Limited,
a company incorporated in England and Wales having its registered office at
264 Banbury Road, Oxford, OX2 7DY – Registered company number: 6695582

www.raintree.co.uk

Editorial credits
Erika L. Shores, editor; Dina Her, designer; Katy LaVigne, production specialist

The Perfect Fundraiser
ISBN: 978 1 3982 0205 4

Printed and bound in India.

Contents

CHAPTER 1
Money for a recording studio

"No, no, no," said Raj. "Throw all of this out. Nobody will buy this junk."

He waved his hand across the row of tables in front of him. "This vase is cracked."

Jez held up a small yellow clock. "What about this?"

"Useless," said Raj. "You can't tell the time on a clock without hands."

"Hey, Jez," said Ari. "Throw it here."

Jez threw the clock, making Ari leap high to catch it.

"Why did you do that?" asked Mia.

"I wanted to see time fly," said Ari.

Raj, Jez, Ari and Mia laughed.

"This fundraiser must be perfect." Raj folded his arms. "If we don't find things to sell, no money, then no school recording studio. I want to record our music and share it with everyone."

Mia smiled. She couldn't wait to use the new microphones, speakers, computer and other equipment.

Jez sighed happily. He played the drums. Ari played the guitar. Of course Raj was the lead singer, and he was excellent. Mia would use the computer to make their band sound so cool.

Mia looked at the piles of boxes and bags that people in the neighbourhood had donated for them to sell. There must be something good there.

"Hey!" Jez fished out a small box. "Who doesn't want a yo-yo?"

"I'll price it," said Raj. "Flat fee for all of them in that box."

"Um," said Mia in her quiet voice. "We'll make more money if we split them up and sell them one-by-one. Kids will love them. How many are there?"

"Twenty," said Jez.

"Ka-ching!" said Raj. "OK, let's hurry up."

They dived into the boxes and bags.

"Cool," said Jez. "Can I have these brand new headphones?"

Raj paused. It was easy to charge as much as you could with strangers but it was different when it was a friend.

7

CHAPTER 2
An interesting find

"I don't want a freebie," said Jez. "How much? Act like you don't know me."

Mia found the price of the headphones on her phone. She showed Jez. "Maybe half?"

"Done!" said Jez.

"Can somebody help me?" Ari held his nose as he dug through a mountain of fabric bags.

Raj joined him. A strong, old, musty smell hit Raj in the face. He took a deep breath and struggled to pick up a striped bag. It was really heavy.

He unzipped it. "Three pairs of hand weights."

"What do you think weighs more?" asked Jez as he sorted through a wooden box of children's toys. "A tonne of feathers or a tonne of bricks?"

"Too easy," said Ari. "Bricks!"

Jez's red face looked ready to explode. "They weigh the same. They both weigh a tonne."

Everyone laughed.

"Good one," said Raj. "But it's nearly one o'clock. Hurry up, everybody."

Raj searched through the mountain of bags. He divided them into a junk pile and a pile they hoped to sell. Raj sorted faster and faster until he was done with his pile.

Raj panted, "Come on, Ari. We want to go home tonight."

Ari shrugged. "OK! I'll speed it up."

Soon only one bag remained.

"Lucky last." Raj swung a pink and blue swirled bag back and forth in his hand. "It's empty, but we can sell the bag."

He flung it towards the sell pile. It made a soft, thudding sound as it fell near Jez, who picked it up.

"Something's inside." He pulled out a black-coloured pen with a lid, which he took off.

The others came over for a look and stared at the metal end.

"Whoa! What is that?" asked Ari.

CHAPTER 3
What is it?

"It's an old fountain pen," said Raj. "My mother owns one that belonged to her mother and her mother before her. Whenever I hold the pen, I always think how my great grandmother once held it."

"How does it work?" asked Jez.

"The metal bit is the nib. You dip it into a bottle of ink and the ink runs up into the barrel, which is the part that holds the ink. Then you write until the ink runs out."

Mia held out her hand. "Can I have a look?"

She looked closely at the cream strip running around the pen's barrel before rubbing it gently against her two front teeth.

"Don't eat it," said Ari.

Mia ignored him and rubbed it against her teeth again.

"Stop it," said Jez. "There could be germs."

"The white band is pearl. My grandmother taught me if you rub pearl against your teeth, real pearl feels gritty rather than smooth." She rubbed the pen with the sleeve of her jumper. "The black's coming off a bit." She held up the pen. The sunlight made it shine.

The others gasped.

"It's gold," said Ari.

"We can sell it and make loads of money for the school," said Mia.

"But should we?" asked Raj.

"You're right," said Mia. "We need to find the owner and return it."

Raj nodded. But how could they find the right owner?

Mia turned the pink and blue swirled bag inside out. There was no label. Somebody must have made it by hand.

Raj thought for a second. "We should try to find out more about the fountain pen. Mum always visits a shop that sells old stuff. It's an antiques shop on Station Street. She buys ink there to sign our birthday cards with her fountain pen. Follow me!"

They raced towards the shop. As they opened the door, a bell rang.

CHAPTER 4
Is it valuable?

A man with curly grey hair and thick glasses stood behind the counter.

Raj frowned. "Where's Mrs Singh?"

"I'm the new owner. Call me Harry."

Raj explained how somebody had mistakenly donated something to their school fundraiser. He showed Harry the fountain pen and asked how much it was worth.

Harry snatched the pen out of Raj's hand. His eyes looked really big behind his glasses. He carefully scratched the black surface with a fingernail. More and more gold appeared. Raj held his breath.

"Junk," said Harry. "It's worthless."

Gently, he placed the pen onto the counter, resting his fingers lightly across it.

"It looks like gold and pearl," said Raj. "Gold is a really valuable metal."

"'Looks' is the right word. Take it from me." Harry stared at the floor beside Raj's foot. "It's fake."

"So we don't need to search for the owner?" asked Jez.

Harry shook his head. "They threw it away, but I'll take it off your hands to help out. People call me Helpful Harry."

Raj gave his friends a quick look.

"I'll give you a couple of quid because it's for a fundraiser," said Harry, lightly tapping his fingers on the pen.

"No!" said Mia loudly.

Raj, Jez and Ari jumped. Mia never talked loudly. She grabbed the pen. Harry gave her a mean look, his forehead dripping with sweat.

"We're leaving," Mia said as she walked outside. The boys trailed after her.

"What? Why?" asked Raj. "Money is money."

"Didn't you see his sweat and how he couldn't look us in the eye?" said Mia. "He was lying. Where's another antiques shop?"

Raj scratched his head. "When I was little, Grandma took me to an antiques shop that I think sold fountain pens. It's around here somewhere. It isn't listed online. I need to remember where it is."

Mia, Ari and Jez lined up behind Raj.
Together they tramped along the streets for
an hour.

CHAPTER 5
Where did it come from?

Jez moaned, "Raj remember harder, before my feet fall off."

Raj peered down a small, dark path between buildings. "Here."

"Let's go," said Ari.

The friends made their way past rubbish bins until they reached a green door. "The Antique Parlour". They stepped inside.

"Hello?" shouted a voice from down the stairs.

A tall woman wearing a pink feather scarf appeared. "I'm Miriam Goldberg. Call me Mimi."

"Hi, Mimi." Raj pulled the fountain pen from its bag. "Please, can you look at this?"

Mimi looked closely at it, before slipping a cloth out of her pocket. She polished the pen as if it were the most valuable object in the world. "It's my special gold cleaning cloth and this is one special gold fountain pen. It's worth a small fortune."

Raj, Mia, Ari and Jez gasped.

"How can a pen be worth so much?" asked Jez.

"This is from a pen manufacturer from abroad," said Mimi. "This pen maker only made 10 pens the year of the company's 100th birthday. They shipped the 10 pens to a few cities around the world. They used only the best gold and silver. I saw one many years ago when my father ran this shop."

"The owner must live around here to have donated stuff to our fundraiser. Would your father remember who bought it?" asked Mia.

"Sadly," said Mimi. "He's passed away."

"Oh, I'm sorry," said Jez.

"I wonder who made the bag," said Raj.

Mimi stared at the pink and blue swirled bag. "My mother sewed me a dress in that material. She bought it from Ms Pallas at the Fabric Barn on Baker Street."

"Thanks," shouted Raj, before racing out onto the pavement and round the corner.

They stopped at a sign saying "Fabric Barn". Together they looked through the dirty, dusty windows. It looked as if nobody had been there for 100 years. Mia wondered if people went in but never came out. She swallowed hard and marched to the door.

CHAPTER 6
Whose is it?

"Can I help you?" Ms Pallas was a tiny woman with short grey hair. She made her way through the stacks of material lying everywhere.

Raj crossed his fingers. Hopefully, she could help them.

Jez held up the bag. "Do you recognize this?"

Her jaw dropped. "That's a blast from the past. I sold that fabric 30 years ago. Luckily, I have a photographic memory. I remember everything I see. Mrs Goldberg bought some to make something for her daughter, Mimi."

Raj sighed. They knew Mimi's mother made a dress.

"And Mrs Marcello used it for curtains. Does that help?"

Mia shook her head sadly.

"Your memory's great," said Jez. "Can you teach me?"

"I was born with it, but you have your own gifts." She clicked her tongue. "I remember something else. I used the leftover material to sew a bag for Ms Langston."

She turned the bag inside out, studying the small stitches sewn along the seams. "That's my work. This belongs to Dalia Langston who lives next door, on the fourth floor."

Raj, Mia, Ari and Jez cheered. Ms Pallas covered her ears, grinning. She asked the children to come back to tell her what happened next. They agreed and ran up the stairs of the building next door.

"Here," puffed Mia, pointing to a nameplate. "Dalia Langston."

Raj knocked loudly on the door.

"Do you need help?" asked a worried-looking woman. "I heard you coming!"

Raj smiled and held up the bag. "Do you recognize this?"

"It's one of the bags I donated to the school fundraiser."

"We found a pen inside."

Ms Langston put a hand on her chest. "After all this time? Is it a gold pen with a pearl band?"

"Exactly that!" said Raj.

"I'm an artist," she said. "I used that pen to draw my first cartoons, but I lost it a few years ago."

Raj passed her the pen. He explained it was a bit black, but she could clean it.

Ms Langston held it gently. Tears filled
her eyes.

Raj, Mia, Ari and Jez smiled.

CHAPTER 7
A perfect ending

Ms Langston told them how her father bought the pen for her 21st birthday from the Antique Parlour. It was made in Switzerland. She thought she had lost it at her 30th birthday picnic and searched the park for days.

She held up the bag. "It was here all the time. Come over next Sunday. I'll draw a picture of your group!"

"Can I make funny faces as it's a cartoon?" asked Jez.

Ms Langston laughed and told him funny faces were encouraged.

Raj looked at his watch. "We'd better go."

"Wait. There's a reward for returning my pen! I would like to give it to your fundraiser."

Raj gasped. "Really?"

Ms Langston nodded.

The kids walked happily back to school. Mia smiled as she imagined the recording studio. Ari dreamed of hearing his guitar recorded and played back again and again.

"Tracking stuff down is exhausting," said Jez, dragging his feet into the school playground.

"Cheer up, Jez," said Raj. "Hopefully, we'll have money left to buy you some drumsticks."

"I feel lucky," said Jez as he stuck his hand into a nearby box.

SNAP! "Owwwwooooow," screamed Jez.

"Don't bother trying out for lead singer." Raj pulled a small mousetrap off Jez's finger. "There's only room for one in the band."

Jez laughed while rubbing his sore finger.

"Guess what this fundraiser is?" asked Raj.

"Perfect!" The four friends shouted as they clapped each other's hands.